VOLUNTEERING

VOLUNTEERING

**A GUIDE
TO SERVING IN THE
BODY OF CHRIST**

LEITH ANDERSON & JILL FOX

ZONDERVAN

Volunteering
Copyright © 2015 by Leith Anderson and Jill Fox

This title is also available as a Zondervan ebook.
Visit www.zondervan.com/ebooks.

This title is also available in a Zondervan audio edition.
Visit www.zondervan.fm.

Requests for information should be addressed to:

Zondervan, 3900 *Sparks Dr. SE, Grand Rapids, Michigan 49546*

Library of Congress Cataloging-in-Publication Data

Anderson, Leith, 1944-
    Volunteering : a guide to serving in the body of Christ / Leith Anderson
and Jill Fox.
        pages cm
    ISBN 978-0-310-51917-1 (softcover)
    1. Voluntarism — Religious aspects — Christianity. I. Title.
BR115.V64A53 2015
    253 — dc23   2015004850

Cover design: Brand Navigation
Cover photo: www.iStockphoto.com
Interior design: Denise Froehlich

Printed in the United States of America

---

15 16 17 18 19 20 /DCI/ 17 16 15 14 13 12 11 10 9 8 7 6 5 4 3 2 1

For Molly and Brooke,
my best friends who never stop believing in me

And for all who volunteer:
you are needed, and never forget that God is using you

Contents

Introduction

HOW TO USE THIS BOOK

You've heard about the need, sensed the call, felt the stirring in your heart to *do* something to help others. You want to serve. You want to volunteer your time and effort toward something worthwhile.

But you also have some doubts. You aren't sure you can do it. Or maybe you've volunteered before, and it just didn't work out the way you had hoped.

This book is for you. It's written for the person who hears about an outreach or a ministry opportunity in the church or community and wants to know more about what's involved, whether it's the right fit, and whether he or she can be successful.

Or maybe you already volunteer, and this book is being used by your leaders as part of a seminar or training workshop. Our hope and prayer is that what you read and learn will inspire you to use your God-given spiritual gifts, your experience, and your talents to do the ministry he has planned for you.

Jill Fox has done the majority of the compiling and writing for this book, so when the pronoun "I" is used, it refers to her. But the content is a true collaboration between the two writers, so both authors' names appear on the cover.

And if you are tasked with leading and training volunteers in your church or nonprofit ministry, we'd like you to know that this is a companion to a more complete guide on the subject, *The Volunteer Church*. Both of the books grew out of the ministry of Leith Anderson and Jill Fox in recruiting and developing volunteers at Wooddale Church in Eden Prairie, Minnesota. Their experience also includes interacting and working with leaders from churches of all sizes and many denominations, as well as seminary students, over many years.

CHAPTER 1

Making the Case

WHY VOLUNTEER?

It was a special night. This wasn't your typical Wednesday evening kids' program. The fourth graders were gathered together on the floor, waiting in anticipation for their guest. The senior pastor was coming to share about his recent travels, visiting several missionaries from the church in different countries. For kids whose idea of a vacation involved a couple of hours in the family minivan, they were fascinated to hear about flying across oceans to faraway places that some had never even heard of.

Ty was one of the inquisitive fourth graders listening carefully as the pastor began to talk about the countries he'd been to and the people he had met. But then the pastor did something that made Ty sit up straight. He handed each of the kids a single coin and said to them, "Your life is like a coin. You can spend it any way you want. But you can only spend it once." Ty sat quietly clutching his coin in his hand. The words continued to circle in his head. That night a seed was planted in Ty's heart and mind. He began wondering whether his life could be used to make a difference, maybe even by serving people who had never heard the gospel.

Ty is now in his thirties, but that night was the beginning of a journey toward dedicating his life to serving God with his whole heart. For him, that meant eventually becoming a missionary. That initial challenge is still a beacon for his life, and the words

11

have been burned into his soul. *Your life is like a coin. You can spend it any way you want. But you can only spend it once.* Those simple words pierced his heart and have set a new course for his life. They helped him see both the freedom and responsibility he'd been given to do something meaningful with his time on earth.

The reality is that all Christians have been given our own "coins," our own set of opportunities and responsibilities, as Jesus described in the parable of the talents. How will we spend them? How will we choose among the possible paths laid out before us?

Our lives are valuable; they matter. Even if we haven't always made wise choices, we still have the chance to use our interests, skills, experiences, and gifts to change the world around us. We can show our families, our friends, and our neighbors how they too can live for Jesus Christ. The question is whether we will seize the opportunities that cross our paths.

And this is not easy. It involves changing how we think and what we do. It means nothing less than becoming like Jesus. I know that sounds like an impossible goal. But let me put it in the simplest of terms: Jesus was the ultimate volunteer. As the eternal Son of God, he volunteered himself for a rescue mission. He became human to serve the whole world, dying on the cross to take the sentence for sin that hangs over all of our lives. Jesus himself declared it this way: "The Son of Man did not come to be served, but to serve, and to give his life as a ransom for many" (Matt. 20:28). This was his mission, the passion that motivated him to live and to die.

The Bible tells us that we are followers of Jesus. We are Christians who are being changed each day to become more like Jesus. And an essential part of becoming like Jesus, the ultimate servant, involves serving others.

Are you interested in becoming more like Jesus? Do you want your life to reflect the life of the ultimate volunteer, Jesus? You are reading this book, which means you are at least somewhat interested. Maybe you're thinking about volunteering. Maybe you're already serving and interested in finding more ways to help others become like Jesus. I'd like to invite you to take a journey, a journey to discover what it means to be a volunteer in your church, in your community, and around the world. And on the way, my hope and prayer is that you will become more like Jesus, discovering the specific opportunities God has in mind for you — the volunteer opportunity with your name written on it!

So where are *you* today? Let's get started by reading through the following categories to see where you fit. This will help you as you process the information in this little book, and it will help your leaders, whether you are looking to volunteer at church or in a parachurch organization, to guide you along the way. Please be assured that whatever category you find yourself in is absolutely fine. Each person reading this book will be at a different place on the journey of volunteering, but know that you are all heading in the same direction. We are all working out how we can grow to become more like Jesus, the ultimate servant.

Categories of Volunteers

1. The "On the Fence, Thinking It Over" Volunteer

You've heard the announcements; you've seen the invitations in the weekly communication at church. They seem to be following you everywhere you go. To volunteer or not to volunteer? It all seems a little scary. What if you don't like it? Will you be stuck doing something you hate? What if someone in a particular group or activity asks you something you can't answer? What if—horrors!—they don't like you? Your concerns are genuine. On the flip side, you've seen others happily and successfully volunteering. You can't help but wonder whether you are missing out on something. And maybe even worse, whether Jesus is missing out on you, missing the skills, talents, energy, creativity, and passion for others you would bring.

2. The "Let Me at 'Em, Can't Wait to Start" Volunteer

You have been watching all the excitement at church, hearing friends talk about their satisfying, fulfilling volunteer situations, and you are champing at the bit to jump in and be a part of the action. You have only one issue: Where do I start? Children's ministry, welcome team, youth, music/worship, helping the elderly, and on and on—which one is right for me? There are so many appealing, interesting choices! You know you are going to love volunteering once you get going, and you want this process to begin moving yesterday!

3. The "I Haven't Found the Right Fit, Maybe They Don't Need Me" Volunteer

You've been trying your hardest, but things just haven't clicked for you. You've attempted to find a place as a volunteer, but the experiences you've had so far haven't worked out the way you'd hoped. To be honest, volunteering has felt more like a chore than a life-giving and encouraging experience. Maybe you've even been tempted to quit or not show up for your serving stint. Volunteering shouldn't remind you of your childhood chores. You haven't found your right fit yet, but you really want to volunteer, to give back. You are on a quest to see if there really is a right fit for you, a role that you'll love, a role that will mean something to those you serve, to you, and to God.

4. The Veteran Volunteer

You've been volunteering for years now, and you still love it. Sure, there are times it's exhausting, but you've seen God do amazing things through you and through other volunteers. You can't imagine not volunteering; it makes you feel alive—closer to God, closer to those with whom you serve, and closer to the ones you serve. As a matter of fact, you love it so much you've even offered to lead a team. You are ready to learn more about recruiting, training, nurturing, and maintaining a group, and you're hoping this book will help you do that.

These are just a few examples of different types of volunteers. We are all at different places when it comes to serving and volunteering. Some of you know you want to volunteer, but you need to take the next couple of steps to find the right spot. For others, it might be about helping to lead a volunteer team in an even stronger direction.

Take some time to think through a few things about volunteering. We have a few questions for you to work through individually or with a group. The goal of this process is for you to feel confident in your decision to volunteer or lead teams of volunteers. We want to make sure you have all the information you need to make good decisions.

Volunteering Is Biblical

Let's begin by looking at what the Bible has to say about volunteering. The Scriptures tell us that God has chosen his people—you and me—to share the transforming message of Jesus Christ with others. Romans 12:4–8 paints a picture of exactly what God was thinking:

> Just as each of us has one body with many members, and these members do not all have the same function, so in Christ we who are many form one body, and each member belongs to all the others. We have different gifts, according to the grace given us. If a man's gift is prophesying, let him use it in proportion to his faith. If it is serving, let him serve; if it is teaching, let him teach; if it is encouraging, let him encourage; if it is contributing to the needs of others, let him give generously; if it is leadership, let him govern diligently; if it is showing mercy, let him do it cheerfully.

This portion from the letter to the Romans clearly shows that each member of the family of God is significant, chosen, and designed to be part of the divine master plan!

When you put your faith in Jesus Christ, you became part of his family, his team, his tribe, his cohort (whatever you want to call it). God expects that you will use your gifts, talents, and abilities for his glory and the advancement of his kingdom. We do all of this to make God look good, for his glory. If you like sports, think of it this way: God didn't sign you up for his team to simply have you to sit on the sidelines of life; he designed you to play. And he has just the right position in mind for you.

Kennedy had the cleats, socks, pants, and hat. She even had the shirt with her name on the back. She looked like a softball player, but she was far from it. This little eight-year-old girl had found herself on a team with a highly competitive coach who wanted to win every game regardless of the needs of the girls on this elementary-school team. Because the coach wasn't sure of Kennedy's abilities, she spent most of her time on the bench, watching softball rather than playing softball. Week after week, it was the same thing. She sat on the hard, metal bench, watching her teammates participating and having fun, wondering when her turn would come. As she sat, something else was happening as well. Kennedy was getting annoyed, agitated, and irritable. She wanted to play. She *knew* she could play. She just needed the chance.

Finally Kennedy's opportunity arrived. One of her teammates was hurt, and just like that, Kennedy was up to bat. As she walked up to the plate, all the frustrations she'd had while sitting on that bench boiled up inside her. Today, she meant business. Kennedy took up her batting stance, just as she had watched her teammates do, perfectly imitating the form she had been taught. She grasped the bat tightly as the softball soared toward home plate, and then she swung at it for dear life. *Crack!* Just like that, the ball went flying into left field, and Kennedy was off running the bases.

After crossing home plate, Kennedy arrived in the dugout and her coach was standing there in shock. She looked at the girl and said, "I didn't know you could hit." Kennedy looked up at her, pushed her hair out of her eyes, straightened her cap, and said in a firm voice, "You never gave me a chance. Of course I can hit!"

Unlike Kennedy, we have a coach who knows we can hit. And instead of keeping us benched, he is nudging us off the bench and into the game. You have a thoughtful and purposeful heavenly coach who created you and made you for something special and unique.

He doesn't want you to miss out on playing the game. He wants and needs you in the game; whether you hit home runs or catch fly balls or bring water to the players, he made you to be part of what he is doing. He's called you to take part in the most important game of all: the game of life. You are a key member of his team.

Questions for Reflection and Discussion

1. Think about your life right now in terms of a softball or baseball game. Are you sitting on the bench, or are you playing the game? How would you describe yourself and your volunteer readiness today?

   _____

2. What are some of the ways you serve others throughout your week at home, at church, and in your workplace? Though we may not be volunteering in formal ways, each of us is involved in serving in some capacity.

   _____

3. What things are you doing that you don't consider to be important or worthy enough to be valuable? The ways you are naturally serving can become stepping stones to something else, opportunities that might stretch you beyond your comfort zone.

   _____

4. What are some of the gifts, talents, and abilities that God has given to you? What are the experiences you've had that God might use? Assuming there are no barriers to serving in a ministry (skill, education, time, etc.), what would you most like to do as a volunteer?

   We'll spend more time thinking about this, but for now, list ways your passions, skills, and experiences might be used by God to help others become a part of God's kingdom and grow as Christians.

   _____

5. What are some ways you have seen God using volunteers in your church? What did you appreciate about these volunteers and the service they performed?

Volunteering Grows Your Faith

Even though eighteen years have passed, Molly can clearly remember Jenny's short blonde hair and her enormous blue eyes. Each time she thinks of Jenny, she also recalls a moment that would change them both forever.

It had been an amazing week at summer camp. And now, as they sat and talked, Jenny looked up at Molly and had a question for her. Jenny said to her counselor, "I want to live for Jesus. How do I do that?" Molly's heart began to beat faster. As a teenage camp volunteer, she didn't feel prepared to answer that question. She understood what Jenny was asking, but she had never answered it before. She took a breath and pointed out a spot for them to sit under a nearby oak tree. The short walk over to the tree gave Molly some time to think.

Molly did her best to explain the gospel to Jenny, and several minutes later, under the shade of the oak tree, Molly saw her little elementary-school camper give her life to Jesus. Molly hugged Jenny after saying the commitment prayer, and as Jenny headed off to her cabin, Molly could hardly catch her breath. It was an indescribable feeling. Overwhelmed and amazed, she sat on the grass and cried. How had God used *her*—just a simple camp counselor—to be part of such a marvelous thing, such a life-changing moment?

That moment changed Jenny's life forever, of course. But the experience of leading someone to know Jesus Christ also changed Molly's life. She knew on that day that following Jesus Christ and sharing his story with others was the best thing in life. Seeing someone come to faith propelled her to move forward in her faith. She wanted to know God more deeply. She wanted to share him more easily, more fully. She wanted to live for him more faithfully. Now, at the age of thirty-four, Molly is still convinced that sharing God's love with others is the best thing in life. It not only transforms the lives of others; it continues to make a profound difference in her own life.

When we volunteer, we become the hands and feet of Jesus. We become the eyes and ears to see or hear of a need, and we follow the nudging of the Holy Spirit to say or do what is necessary. And ultimately this pushes us forward in our faith. As volunteers, we get to experience things we never would if we didn't jump in to be part of it all. Through his church, his family, God is unfolding his plans, building his kingdom, and developing and expanding his mission in this world beyond what we can imagine. As volunteers, we get to play in the greatest game ever played. Instead of sitting in the stands, it's like being in the state finals and feeling the adrenaline flow. It's getting to stand hand in hand with the cast after the curtain call and celebrating because you did something great together—you pulled off a great performance.

You and I are invited to play a part in a grand story that God has been writing since the creation of the world. It's a story that began in a garden and led to a man dying on a cross. It's the story of new life, of resurrection, and of how the rescue mission of God is continuing today through you and through me. We are a part of the story of Jesus Christ transforming lives. And God uses many different people in a variety of ways to write this story. Your part could be feeding the hungry at a shelter and talking with them while the rest of the world turns a blind eye to their needs. Or you may be the one who spends hours reciting memory verses with third graders so they can remember what is true—truth that combats the lies they are told on the playground, truth that they may still recall thirty years from now.

Or maybe your part in the story involves opening the front door for the first-time visitor and welcoming him or her to the church. You may be visitors' first introduction to Jesus Christ, even though they might not realize it.

We all have a role to play in the story, a place on the team. These are just a few of the ways we can get involved. Don't just be an observer. Volunteering is how we grow as Christians, it's how the local church fulfills its mission, and it is how God is accomplishing his purposes in this world.

Questions for Reflection and Discussion

1. When was the last time you felt like you grew in your faith? How did you feel while it was happening? How do you see it now, as you look back on it?

2. Have you ever been part of a group—whether in church or someplace else—where you did something you really enjoyed with a group, all together? What did that feel like? What did you accomplish together?

3. What makes you nervous about volunteering? Have you felt this apprehension in similar situations? What are some ways you were able to overcome it and be successful, despite how you felt?

The Purpose and the Reward

Wake up. Shower. Dress. Eat. Drive. Work. Drive. Eat. Sleep. Repeat. Repeat. Repeat. Have you ever felt like your life is just one big routine? Have you ever asked yourself if this is all there is to life? What is your true purpose? Many others struggle with these questions as well.

Whatever your routine might be, your life can have meaning and purpose. Volunteering is one way you can quickly take a life that seems purposeless, boring, and insignificant and turn it around. Consider Victoria's story. Victoria was an accountant in her late thirties, and she seemed to have it all together. She had gone to college, pursued a postgraduate degree, and landed a great job in her field. She had hoped that finding success in her chosen career would give her life meaning, but inside she felt empty. One Sunday, in the hope of discovering something to give her life greater meaning than what she was finding at work, she checked a box on the back of the church information card. It had the words Student Ministries written next to it. *I'll just see what this is all about*, she told herself. *Then I can decide if I'm interested ... or not.*

It wasn't too long before she found herself standing in a sea of giggling middle-school girls. And most surprising of all, she found she enjoyed it! Victoria never would have guessed that a group of young girls could fill a part of her life that had been empty for years. For the first time in a long time, she felt as if she had a new purpose. She was giving part of her life to others, investing herself in ways that truly mattered to her and to God. Walking alongside these early teens, loving them, showing Jesus to them—this was what she had been made to do.

As if finding a renewed purpose in life weren't enough, there were also surprising rewards for Victoria herself. She was blessed by handwritten notes describing why she was "the best leader ever" and hugs on Sunday mornings from overly perfumed thirteen-year-olds. All of this reminded her that she mattered and was making a difference.

Think about a time when you felt a strong sense of purpose in your life. Is that something that happens frequently, or do you sit at your desk wishing you were doing something with more purpose and more importance? Maybe you know exactly what you are called to do. Or maybe life seems like it is just passing you by. While we all experience moments where life is dull, and there are ordinary times where we are simply getting through the day, the deeper question is still worth asking: does your life have a sense of purpose? Why are you here?

For many people, that sense that "I'm doing what I'm supposed to do" often comes when they are volunteering. As a church leader, I love seeing a new person get connected at our church and finding new meaning in life. And this can be your experience as well. Perhaps it is talking with a visitor at the welcome center and listening to the story that has brought him or her to you. Or it can be watching the twenty-year-old man who is part of the disabilities ministry and hearing him share that your encouraging note gave him the confidence he needed for his first day at his first job. Those are the moments in life that make it all seem worth it. They give you a sense of purpose, and they are extremely rewarding. Those are the times when you sense that you are being Jesus' hands and feet in the world.

People spend much of their lives looking for fulfillment in their circumstances. We spend money on a house, hoping that when we walk into it each day it will be rewarding—a refuge for us, a reminder of all our hard work. We buy the newest toys in the hope of "moving up" and finding acceptance from the "right" people. We are constantly looking to fill our lives with different things to help us find security.

The reality is that the things that are most rewarding here on earth simply can't be bought. The most rewarding experiences come by *giving*, not getting. It's the reward you receive in giving your week to volunteer with vacation Bible school, seeing those first graders repeat John 3:16 with full voice and bright eyes. It's being the volunteer who worked in the gardens at church for hours on Saturday and watching families sit together in that space, enjoying the beauty around them on Sunday. It's getting a note in the mail from someone in the congregation, letting you know that the words you sang helped to heal a part of her life that was deeply hurt. Those are true rewards. Those are the rewards that will be poured into and through you as you volunteer. And the best reward of all is hearing God say, "Well done, good and faithful servant."

Questions for Reflection and Discussion

1. Think about some of the experiences in your life that have been particularly meaningful and filled with a sense of purpose. Why do you think they felt that way?

_____

2. What are some of the rewards you would like to receive out of volunteering?

Growing as a Community

Cade wandered into the church building, not really sure even how he found his way there. He sat all alone in the front row, waiting for the service to start. Someone on the pastoral staff saw him sitting there, so she made her way over to say hello, welcome him, and let him know that if he had any questions he could let her know. Soon afterward, a few others joined him in the chairs by him, shook his hand, and asked his name. Cade wasn't expecting anyone to notice him, let alone welcome him. Something happened that evening at church, something unanticipated. Cade sensed that God was calling him to *that* place, and the people there confirmed that this was where he belonged.

The people Cade met that night didn't know much of his story. But soon he was involved with the welcome team and jumping in to participate on the church mission trips. As Cade served with other volunteers, he began to share his story with them, a story of powerful life change. Gradually the facts came out. Cade's life had been controlled by all the wrong things, like the drugs and pornography that had filled his life and led him down a destructive path, and he had been filled with loneliness. It was on that night when he walked into that church service that things started to change. Cade found God, and his life began to transform. Not only did he find the Savior he needed, he found a new community. He found friends who loved him and cared for him as they served alongside him.

God created us to be social beings in his image, and when we serve together, it builds strong relationships between us. As we serve with others, we learn each other's stories. Powerful bonds develop because of our mutual care and concern for those in the ministry area where we are volunteering. This shared passion and shared purpose leads to close friendships.

And because we are serving in the church, the family of God, we know that what we are doing isn't just making a difference today; it has implications for eternity. We make new friends—people to care for, love, and do life with.

Questions for Reflection and Discussion

1. When was the last time you felt really cared for by a person you did not know? How can you do that for someone else? How can you pay it forward?

   _____

2. When was the last time you cared for a group of people in your church or in the community? How did you feel about that experience? Would you do it again? Why or why not?

Make a Difference

The room full of people was quiet in a way it never had been before. People sat riveted as the woman told her story, their faces filled with expressions of shock, horror, grief, and frustration as she shared her experience in the sex-trafficking industry, having men and women sexually abuse her for money. It was heartbreaking to hear of the terrible wrongs and the great evil she had faced, and the audience knew they would never forget what this bold and brave woman was sharing with them.

As her presentation came to an end, the speaker looked around the room and gave a challenge to the young adults listening. She told them that they could make a difference. They could be a part of ending modern-day slavery, this global horror involving countless numbers of children and adults. She gave them specific, simple examples of how they could make a difference in shutting it down, and she pointed them to a table where they could sign up to help.

As she concluded her talk, a wave of people swept across the room toward the table. Their hearts obviously were breaking, and they wanted to help make a difference. Sure, they knew they couldn't change everything by themselves, but they knew they could volunteer to serve one or two victims, educate others about sex trafficking and the horrors of it, or volunteer with organizations rescuing the victims. There was something an individual could do to commit to the cause.

That's what volunteering is all about. Few of us will be involved in leading sweeping global movements that transform cultures. But we, even as individuals, can do the small, simple things that make a difference in the lives of people around us. We can contribute our part in righting the wrongs and injustices of the world.

Let me encourage you: if you are troubled by the pain and the poverty in the world, you can do something! If you are bothered by the number of young men growing up without fathers, you can be a mentor to one or more of them. If your heart breaks for the children who go to bed hungry each night, you can volunteer for a food drive and help stock food shelves.

What is there in the world that needs to change? What have you heard or learned about that makes your heart break? You don't have to sit back and merely watch injustices, sorrows, poverty, loneliness, and other distresses of life continue. As a volunteer, you can help make a difference.

Question for Reflection and Discussion

1. What makes your heart break? What injustices are you aware of that you would like to help alleviate or see eliminated?

CHAPTER 2

Finding Your Fit

To my mother, they looked like a pair of boots you'd wear on a construction site. But I knew that having these boots would complete my middle-school wardrobe. Everyone was wearing them, and I desperately needed them. As I waited for the sales clerk to bring out a pair in my size, I could picture myself walking through the lunchroom, my classmates staring at them with admiration.

Then the clerk brought me the bad news. They didn't carry my size. They had a pair half a size smaller, but that was it. I grabbed the box from him and pulled out a boot. With all my might I crammed my size-five foot into that too-small boot. I stood up and walked around as my mom stared at me with those eyes, the ones that said, *I don't think this will work, honey.* And then she asked the inevitable question: "Do they fit?" I didn't care whether they fit. I knew I had to have them. So I gave a loud and definite "Yes!" So my mom asked me again, "Do they really feel good?" How do you tell your mom that you will die if you don't get these boots right now? How do you let her know that the boys at school just *have* to notice you, and these are the boots that will make that happen? Well, you lie and say they feel great.

One week later, I found myself limping down the hallway on my way to choir. I was in agony, blisters covering my feet.

The boots were a horrible fit, and they were incredibly painful to wear.

Desire can take you only so far. You need to find shoes that fit, or the experience can be painful. And shoes aren't the only items in life that can be a painful fit. Volunteer roles can be painful as well. Maybe you've been asked to give the announcements, but you know that cottonmouth is your worst enemy. Or you're placed in the nursery, but holding babies just isn't really your thing. Or perhaps you've found yourself on a retreat, caught in the crossfire of junior-high boys shooting water at each other, and all you can think about is packing your bags and leaving.

Fit matters. It matters a lot when it comes to volunteering. While the service you perform won't always be a cakewalk and there will be times of struggle and difficulty, your volunteer role should be life-giving. If it's not, and you are constantly drained by the experience, you'll no doubt give up. Sometimes people have this experience and vow never to volunteer again out of fear they'll end up in another unsuitable fit. (Please don't quit; talk to your leader for help in figuring out something else.) When you volunteer, you want to find a role that feels like you are doing what God has called you to do.

Why does this matter? Because when those inevitable bumps in the road come your way, you won't be as overwhelmed. If you sense God's calling and feel that this is where you belong, you'll push through the hard times because you know you were made for this ministry.

Take a moment right now to stop and say a quick prayer, asking the Lord to help you use the tools in the next section to help you discover your gifts and find your fit.

Spiritual Gifts

First of all, do you know what your spiritual gift is? If you don't, I have some good news for you. When you became a follower of Jesus Christ, you were given a gift from God for his purposes in the kingdom. The gift God gives you is for something specific, something he wants you to do, a part to play in God's story. And once you know your gift, you can have confidence that you are heading in the right direction and serving in the right ministry areas. You'll have something great to offer—great in God's eyes, even if it might seem rather small and ordinary in the world's view.

To begin, think of a spiritual gift as a job or a responsibility, something you do for others. There are lots of tasks to be done in every church and related organizations, and God gives different gifts to different Christians to cover them all. The Bible uses the illustration of a human body to describe how all of the gifts work together in the church. Like the various organs and parts of the human body, each of us has a purpose and function. The parts of the body cannot be swapped around. They can't do each other's jobs (1 Corinthians 12). The job of the heart is to pump blood, and so the heart has the ability to expand and contract in order to pump. The job of the eyes is to see, so they have the ability to sense light rays and transmit to the brain. The job of ears is to hear, so they have the ability to sense sound waves, transform them into electrical impulses, and transmit them to our brains.

Hearts can't hear. Ears can't pump blood. And that's the way it is supposed to be. The job assignments and the abilities are perfectly matched. The Bible tells us that this is the way God has designed his church to function. There are some with the job of evangelism, some with the job of teaching, and some with the job of shepherding. Each job is unique, and with each job, the Holy Spirit provides the ability to do the job.

Many Spiritual Gifts, Many to Put Them to Use

Most of the New Testament teaching about spiritual gifts is spelled out in four passages: 1 Corinthians 12–14; Romans 12; Ephesians 4; and 1 Peter 4.

Depending on how the gifts are counted, there are at least nineteen separate gifts:[1]

- Apostle
- Prophet
- Evangelist
- Shepherding
- Teaching
- Exhortation
- Knowledge

- Wisdom
- Helps
- Hospitality
- Giving
- Government
- Showing Mercy
- Faith

- Discernment
- Miracles
- Healing
- Speaking in Tongues
- Interpretation of Tongues

Yes, there are some differing theological understandings about some of the gifts, but don't let those differences hinder what we can be sure about:

1. *Every Christian has one.* Every Christian has been given at least one spiritual gift, and most have multiple gifts, although none of us has all the gifts (Eph. 4:7; 1 Cor. 12:7, 11). Sometimes gifts overlap. Just as eyes can "hear" by reading subtitles in a movie or hands can "talk" with sign language, some gifts can substitute for another in unusual circumstances. But the normal way of understanding is that each spiritual gift is called to a specific job, just as each human organ serves a specific function.

2. *Gifts are empowered by the Holy Spirit.* Spiritual gifts are from God. Spiritual gifts are not the same as talents, although there may be alignment. The main difference is that spiritual gifts are jobs in the body of the church that are supernaturally empowered by the Holy Spirit. Paul explains in 1 Corinthians 12:11 that "all these are the work of one and the same Spirit, and he distributes them to each one, just as he determines."

In a healthy human body every organ does what it is designed to do, and that makes for a wonderful fulfillment of God's design. If one organ malfunctions, the whole body suffers. Yes, you can live without a hand, eye, ear, or foot, but the ideal is when we have them all and they all do what they are designed to do. Likewise, in a healthy church, every Christian has been gifted by the Holy Spirit to do one or more jobs. When all of these gifts are functioning as designed, it is a wonderful fulfillment of God's plan. If an evangelist doesn't evangelize, a teacher doesn't teach, or a helper doesn't help, the church doesn't suddenly die, but it's not as strong and healthy as God intends it to be.

As you have just read all this and are wondering what your spiritual gift is, take a moment right now and walk through a brief assessment. This will be a good start in identifying what areas of ministry might work for you. Simply answer the questions and circle the bullet points that apply to you. If you have questions, use the Scripture references to help you better understand each spiritual gift. And even if you have a pretty good idea of what your gift is, let me encourage you to take the assessment. Your particular experiences and circumstances change over the course of a lifetime, and sometimes God adds new gifts to the ones he has already given you. Here you go!

Spiritual Gifts Assessment

1. What is your understanding of a spiritual gift?

    _____
    _____
    _____
    _____
    _____

2. Read 1 Corinthians 12:4–11. How and when do you get your own
    spiritual gift(s)?

    _____
    _____
    _____
    _____
    _____

3. List the spiritual gifts that you read about in these Scriptures.
    Romans 12:4–8

    _____
    _____

    1 Corinthians 12:7–10

    _____
    _____

    Ephesians 4:11

    _____
    _____

4. Why does God give us these gifts?

   _____

   _____

   _____

   _____

   _____

5. When you become a Christian God calls you to _____
   (1 Peter 2:9).

6. God created you to do good _____ (Eph. 2:10).

7. You each have special _____ that can be used in unique
   ways (Rom. 12:7 – 8).

8. When all of us together use our gifts, it builds the body of
   _____ (Eph. 4:11 – 13).

Descriptions of the Gifts

As you read through the descriptions of the following spiritual gifts, circle
the bullet points that you feel describe you or apply to you.

Apostle

Ability and responsibility to be sent by Jesus Christ to establish his church
where it has not been (Mark 3:14 – 19; Mark 6:30; Gal. 1:1; Eph. 2:20; Acts
2:43; 2 Cor. 12:12; 1 Thess. 2:6).

- You care deeply about people hearing and believing the gospel.
- Starting a new church or a new ministry in another country or culture
  moves your spirit.
- You are able to relate well with people of other cultures.
- Being in places you've never been before intrigues you.

Prophet

Ability and responsibility to effectively speak God's message (Eph. 4:11–12;
1 Cor. 14:1; Eph. 2:20; 1 Cor. 14:3; Acts 15:32 *Effect of prophecy, 1 Cor.
14:3, 24–25 *Effect of prophecy, 1 Cor. 14:29–33 *Rules for prophecy,
Rom. 12:6).

- You often are able to speak the truth with love and persuasion.
- You see the present clearly in relation to God's Word, and it may give
  you insight for the future.
- You feel responsible to speak what God has inspired you to say, in line
  with the Bible.

Evangelist

Ability and responsibility to effectively communicate the good news of
salvation in Jesus Christ (Eph. 4:11; Acts 8:4–6, 26–40 *Phillip is called
"evangelist" in Acts 21:8—What did he do? 1 Cor. 15:3–6 *What is the
essence of the gospel? 2 Tim. 4:5).

- You are moved to build relationships with those who do not know
  Jesus Christ.
- You find it easy to share your faith.
- You would enjoy being on an outreach team, whether local or beyond.

Shepherding

Ability and responsibility to spiritually care for and guide God's people (Eph.
4:11–12; 1 Peter 1–5 *Expectations: Who is called "shepherd"? Heb. 13:20;
1 Peter 2:25; 5:4, John 21:15–19; Acts 20:28–31).

- You enjoy mentoring, developing, and seeing people grow.
- You appreciate opportunities to care for people and their needs.
- You could take on the challenge of leading a small group.

Teaching

Ability and responsibility to effectively communicate God's truth so others are equipped to believe and to minister (Eph. 4:11–14 *Results of gift of teaching? Rom. 12:7 *What should a person with the gift of teaching do? Heb. 5:12; 1 Tim. 5:17).

- You are delighted when others understand the truths of God you have shared.
- You appreciate the process of learning and studying God's Word and explaining it to others.
- You may find it life-affirming to teach a class that will help others grow in their faith.

Exhortation

Ability and responsibility to come alongside and provide encouragement, strength, stability, confrontation, consolation, or help (Rom. 12:6–8 *How is exhortation to be done? 1 Thess. 2:11; 5:14 *What was the context of these exhortations? 1 Thess. 2:11–12; 2 Thess. 3:12; 2 Tim. 4:1–4; 1 Peter 5:1–2 *What is the basis of exhortation? Rom. 15:4).

For this gift, take a deeper look at what the Bible teaches. How did these people use the gift of exhortation?

Paul: Acts 14:21–22; 16:40; 20:1; 20:17–23

_____

_____

Judas and Silas: Acts 15:31–32

_____

_____

Peter: 1 Peter 5:1–2

_____

_____

God: 2 Corinthians 1:3−7

_____

_____

- You find yourself wanting to encourage others.
- You may enjoy one-on-one discipling and mentoring.
- You enjoy counseling others.

Knowledge

Ability and responsibility to investigate and systematize facts related to God's revealed truth in the Bible (1 Cor. 12:8; Matt. 16:17 *What is the source of knowledge? 1 Cor. 13:1−13 *What is the relationship of knowledge to love? 1 Cor. 8:1 *What is the danger of knowledge?)

- You appreciate digging deeper and learning biblical truths in detail.
- You may enjoy teaching or taking a class on the Bible.
- You are able to explain biblical truths from what you have studied in the Scriptures.

Wisdom

Ability and responsibility to demonstrate insight in interpreting and under-standing biblical truth (1 Cor. 12:8; 1:24, 30; 2:6−16 *How does spiritual wisdom differ from natural wisdom? James 3:13−18 *Effects of true wisdom? James 1:5; Acts 6:3; 1 Cor. 6:5).

- People may come to you for counsel related to spiritual issues.
- You are able to make good decisions while applying biblical truth to life's challenges.
- You are not daunted by difficult situations, because you can find solutions from the Bible.

Speaking in Tongues

Ability and responsibility to speak in a language that was never learned (*What was the first instance of tongues in the New Testament? Describe what happened. Acts 2:1 – 13. *Define "speaking in tongues" from Acts 2:1 – 13. *Describe how this gift served as a sign to unbelievers: Acts 2:1 – 13; Acts 10:44 – 46; Acts 19:1 – 7. *What are some functions of the gift of speaking in tongues? 1 Cor. 14:4 – 5; 14:22. *What are the rules for speaking in tongues? 1 Cor. 14:26 – 40. *Is speaking in tongues a spiritual gift? 1 Cor. 12:10, 28).

- You have the ability to pray in a language you have never spoken or heard before.
- You believe speaking in tongues is done so others will come to know Jesus Christ.
- When this happens, you believe it pushes you to step out in your faith.

Interpretation of Tongues

Ability and responsibility to hear the words spoken in tongues and then communicate them to others in a language the listeners will understand (*Is interpretation of tongues one of the New Testament spiritual gifts? 1 Cor. 12:10. *Was interpretation always necessary when there was public speaking in tongues? Acts 2:4 – 8; 10:44 – 48. *Why was interpretation of tongues important? 1 Cor. 14:5. *Is the gift of interpretation given to the same person who has the gift of speaking in tongues? 1 Cor. 12:10; 14:5, 13, 27 – 28. *What should be done if speaking in tongues occurs, but there is no one to interpret? 1 Cor. 14:28).

- The purpose behind interpreting tongues is to edify the church.
- You desire this to avoid confusion in the church.
- You provide the interpretation in a way that is orderly and not divisive.

Helps

Ability and responsibility to give needed assistance and support to others (1 Cor. 12:28 *Only explicit New Testament reference. How do the following verses relate—or not—to this gift? Rom. 12:7. Same gift, different name? Luke 10:40; Acts 19:22; 1 Cor. 16:15; 1 Thess. 5:14).

- You are inclined toward working behind the scenes.
- You may want to volunteer with new ministries to get things set up.
- You love assisting others, especially when using your spiritual gifts.

Hospitality

Ability and responsibility to provide welcome, friendship, fellowship, food and/or lodging, especially to newcomers and strangers (1 Peter 4:9–10, *How might hospitality be misused? 1 Peter 4:9; Rom. 12:9–13 *Who might be the unusual recipients of our hospitality? Heb. 13:1–2).

- You enjoy making people feel welcome, whether to your home or church.
- You may love being a part of the greeting ministry.
- You appreciate being able to create a warm and caring atmosphere.
- You enjoy entertaining in your home.

Giving

Ability and responsibility to give materially to the Lord and his work with unusual generosity and joy (Rom. 12:8; 2 Cor. 9:1–7; 8:2–5; 1 Cor. 16:2; Acts 4:34–37; Acts 5:1–11; Eph. 4:28; Matt. 6:3; 1 Cor. 13:3; Phil. 4:14–20).

- You find joy in providing the resources to help ministry happen.
- You may look for ways you can give more.
- You attempt to manage your money well in order to give liberally.
- You are moved to support another missionary.

Government

Ability and responsibility to determine God's goals and guide the body of Christ to the fulfillment of those goals (Mark 10:42–45; 1 Tim. 3:1–7; Titus 1:5–9; 1 Peter 5:2–3; 1 Tim. 5:17; 1 Thess. 5:12; Heb. 13:7, 17, 24).

- You may enjoy strategic planning.
- You look forward to leading a ministry team.
- You have special skills in developing systems for accomplishing a goal.
- You may be able to cast a vision.

Showing Mercy

Ability and responsibility to feel compassion for those in pain and take action to alleviate the hurt (Rom. 12:8 *What is the key characteristic of proper exercise of this gift? Examples: Acts 2:44–45; James 2:15–16; Acts 9:36; 1 Thess. 5:14; Mark 9:41, *Why is the particular emphasis on action, not just attitude? Luke 10:25–35; James 2:14–17).

- You notice others who need to know how much God loves and cares for them.
- You feel for those who are suffering and want to help.
- You may enjoy being a support-group leader or volunteering at food shelves.
- You care deeply about those who may be ignored by others.

Faith

Ability and responsibility to confidently determine the will and the purpose of God for his work and to believe God will accomplish it, even when it looks impossible (1 Cor. *What is faith? Heb. 11:1 *Describe how faith was exercised. Heb. 11).

- You strongly believe in the power of prayer.
- You encourage others to trust God when they have doubts.
- You believe God will keep his promises regardless of circumstances.
- You may appreciate being a volunteer in a prayer ministry.

Discernment

Ability and responsibility to distinguish between the spirit of truth and the spirit of error (How did Peter exercise discernment? Acts 5:1 – 11; 1 Cor. 12:10 *What are Christians to do? 1 John 4:1 – 6; 1 Thess. 5:21).

- Your first impressions of people or situations are typically reliable.
- You can often judge between good and evil.
- You may know when someone is being a phony before others.

Miracles

Ability and power to authenticate God's Word through supernatural acts (1 Cor. 12:10, 28, *What was the primary purpose of New Testament miracles? John 20:30 – 31, *What are examples of New Testament miracles? John 2:1 – 11; 6:1 – 14; 6:15 – 21; 11:1 – 14; Acts 9:36 – 42, *Who performed New Testament miracles besides Jesus? 2 Cor. 12:12, *Is performing miracles a gift for all of God's great leaders? John 10:41).

- You believe strongly that God works through miracles.
- You've seen supernatural answers to prayers.
- You have been involved in a supernatural act (miracle).

Healing

The ability and responsibility to make sick people well (*Who is the greatest recipient and exerciser of this gift? Matt. 9:35 *List lessons and principles from stories of apostolic healings, Acts 3:6 – 8; 5:15 – 16; 28:8 – 9; *Is the person with the gift of healing always able to heal all sickness?

Acts 28:8–9; Phil. 2:25–27; 1 Tim. 5:23; 2 Tim. 4:20; *Why is there divine healing? John 9:1–3; *To what extent is the exercise of the gift of healing dependent upon the faith of the person who is sick? Acts 3:1–10).

- You pray frequently for the sick.
- You may enjoy being on a visitation team.
- You have been used by the Lord in healing others who are physically, spiritually, or emotionally sick.

Your Spiritual Gifts

1. After you have read through the list of gifts and circled the ones that you feel best apply to you and your interests, write down the gifts that seem to be the best match. What spiritual gifts did you discover that you are currently using?

   _____

   _____

   _____

   _____

   _____

2. Was there anything in the assessment that surprised you? If you aren't sure about a particular gift, be sure to talk with leaders at your church about your questions. Once you have a sense of your God-given gift or gifts, take some time to pray that God will give you discernment as you explore how to use your gifts.

   _____

   _____

   _____

   _____

   _____

3. Write down any ideas you have about where and how you might use your spiritual gifts.

    _____

    _____

    _____

    _____

    _____

Talents and Skills

A little rural church in Iowa had a dream, one that included reaching new people for God in their community. But how would they do it? Where would they find the resources? And who would be involved? The first step was to assess who they wanted to reach, then what the church members could contribute toward that goal. After answering these questions, a vision began to take shape. They would begin by building a go-kart track, then they would have some races and organize a car show. All of this was guaranteed to please a crowd in rural Iowa.

Doing this might sound like a daunting task to you. But that wasn't the case for this congregation. Why? Their members were largely made up of farmers who had the talents and skills to accomplish these tasks. They were already attending stock car races on Friday nights, and they were equipped to make mechanical adjustments to just about anything with an engine.

When the big day arrived, the church hosted an outstanding event. They redesigned the parking lot, transforming it into a go-kart track. The turnout for the car show was impressive. Not only did people from the town turn up, they experienced community together as a church in a unique and fresh way. The church learned that the whole event was successful because people were using their God-given talents and skills to serve together. Some of them had helped with the mechanics and construction of the track. Some had organized the food. Others were in charge of advertising. The list went on and on, each person contributing his or her individual skills to create an amazing outcome, and a whole lot of people who hadn't come to church were introduced to God's people in a memorable way, a way that would bring them back.

What are your skills and talents? Make a list. Write down what you do — the things you do every day as well as the occasional activities and skills that might be a good fit with your church's ministries and programs. Look at your church with fresh eyes and try to envision how you can offer these skills and talents that God gave to you for his use. Need some examples to get started? Do you ...

- sing or play an instrument?
- enjoy organizing and bringing order out of chaos?
- have skills with computers or technology?
- have an eye for decorating?
- enjoy landscaping and gardening?
- find you can fix almost anything?
- like to plan events and have some skill at it?
- enjoy cooking and baking?
- like to play and/or organize sporting events?

This is just a start. What are your talents and skills?

_____

_____

_____

_____

_____

Ask Someone Else

So now you should have an idea of what your spiritual gifts are and a list of your talents and skills. Your next step is confirmation. You should find someone who knows you well and ask him or her for input. Honestly, at times we need a little help assessing ourselves, and others who know us best are just right for doing this. Make sure you ask whether your friend sees these spiritual gifts, skills, and talents in you. This person may even recognize something you haven't thought of. This is a vital step in your journey toward discovering your best fit.

Who are some of the people in your life you can ask? Family? Friends? Church leaders?

_____

_____

_____

_____

_____

So What's Next?

You've listed your spiritual gifts and talents and skills. You've confirmed them with those who know you well. Now it's time to volunteer. Reflecting on all you've learned about yourself, and thinking about your church or the local outreach organizations in your community, what sounds intriguing to you? Think of all the places where you see people volunteering. Is there something you've thought about? Is there a place where you might be able to serve, using all that God has given you? Jot down a few ideas.

_____

_____

_____

_____

_____

If you still have questions, that's fine. Talk with someone you're most comfortable with at your church. If you don't have questions right now, let's keep going.

No-Strings-Attached Observing

Remember the illustration at the beginning of this chapter? You don't want to limp along in a certain volunteer role, serving in a place that doesn't seem to work well with your personality, skills, and gifts. So how can you determine whether a volunteer role fits you? How can you be assured that a position is right for you? Let me say up front that no one can give you a guarantee, but the truth is that you will be much more likely to find your place if you try it out. If you've never served in an area before, you can't know for sure whether it is a good fit. Give it a try, but before you commit to leading the junior-high ministry for the next ten years, you might want to try a few meetings and talk to others in that ministry. You can say something like this when you talk to your staff leader or volunteer leader: "I'd like to check out this ministry area and talk with other volunteers before I make a decision."

This is totally acceptable. You are about to make a big commitment. It's important that you make an informed decision. When you walk into a room filled with kids, does it feel like a place that gives you energy? When you stand with a welcome-team member greeting each person who comes in the door, do you feel like this is life-giving or life-taking? And remember that you may not feel this immediately. The real question is whether, over time, you sense that this is something God wants you to do. Do you find yourself caring about the people, enjoying the time you spend there, and wanting to learn more about the ministry? If the answer is yes, you've found your fit.

After you've checked out one or more options, then you'll be ready to decide. Remember, you are looking for a good fit, something you'll want to stick with, not something you'll want to run from in a month—or less!

CHAPTER 3

Teams Are Tops

Alexa leaned against the column near the airport gate. Those obnoxiously bright green shirts with the neon yellow letters on them could not be missed—and that was intentional. After all, there is nothing worse than losing a high-school student in an airport on a mission trip. Alexa watched some of the braver boys positioning themselves near the girls they thought were cute. She watched others wishing they were that brave. Alexa loved them all. She loved them for the quirks, talents, and the small things that made each one unique. But as she stood there, she was also thinking about the news she had not yet shared with them. She soon would be leaving her leadership position with the senior-high ministry because she felt God was calling her in another direction.

As other travelers passed her by on their way to their next destination, Alexa wished she could stop the clock. How would she be able to leave this group of teens? Who else would be there to hug them on their bad days? Who would listen to them talk about their breakups or failed tests? Who would cheer them on at their games and concerts? These students needed her. Through teary eyes, Alexa saw Mr. Collins, the fifty-year-old teddy bear who had volunteered with her since she had started the ministry. Mr. Collins had somehow managed to wrangle the group into a perfect circle. *Now that's impressive*, she thought. Organizing high-schoolers can be like herding cats. A few minutes later, Alexa listened as he led the group through the possible highs and lows of the trip they were about to begin.

In that instant, it struck Alexa that her students would be just fine. They would be more than fine. As much as she loved these kids, she had somehow forgotten that they weren't *just* hers. They needed more than one person in their corner, and they had that in the other leaders, in people like Mr. Collins. Others would step up after she was gone, she knew. She couldn't help but feel a little foolish for her naivete. Yes, the students loved her, and she loved them, but as she looked beyond herself, she saw that there were others who could take her place.

Alexa had wrongly concluded, as most of us do at some point, that we are *essential* to the little piece of God's work that we have been called to do. We are human, and when we find something we deeply love that gives us joy, it's normal to feel this way. Yet as much as we love what we do, the reality is that we can't do everything on our own, nor should we. God hasn't designed us to serve alone. We need others. God created us as relational beings because he made us in his image, and our God of love knows we need others for support, care, and love, and to get things accomplished.

Consider this verse from Ecclesiastes. I think it paints a perfect picture of why teamwork is both biblical and required:

> Two are better than one, because they have a good return for their work: If one falls down, his friend can help him up. But pity the man who falls and has no one to help him up! Also, if two lie down together, they will keep warm.

But how can one keep warm alone? Though one may be overpowered, two can defend themselves. A cord of three strands is not quickly broken.

—ECCLESIASTES 4:9–12

Why It Takes a Team

There are volunteer roles where one person serves, but more often than not, a team is needed. And there are good reasons for this.

1. Groups working together can accomplish more in a shorter time.
2. Teams are made up of individuals with different gifts and abilities.
3. Working together means greater satisfaction and greater reward.
4. A team can solve problems more quickly and effectively.
5. A group can help replace volunteers.

Teams Accomplish More

More good things happen when people work together as a team. This is true in almost every area of life. Want to serve more people at the food shelter each week? Find some more volunteering hands. Want to do a Christmas musical as a community outreach? You will need singers and actors and people to support them.

Jesus understood this. He was the ultimate recruiter. He had a vision to reach the world, but he didn't just set out on his own. He began with a team of twelve. Were they perfect people? No. Were they all the same? No. But they all caught his vision, and they wanted to be on his team. And while Jesus was out teaching the crowds, they were watching him, learning how to be his followers, learning how to work together. These were important lessons they would need to apply when he was no longer with them in person.

Jesus gives us a clue about how we need to think as volunteers. Don't just think of yourself, doing it all alone. Ask yourself: *Who can I add to the circle so we can do more?* I grew up in a small church, and I know this idea can seem overwhelming when you don't have very many people to begin with. But even adding one more person to a team can make a huge difference. So as you are volunteering, look around and ask yourself who else might want to be part of what God is doing.

Teams Have Diverse Gifts and Abilities

Having more people in your group expands your potential for good due to sheer people power, but it also expands the team through additional gifts and abilities. One of the best teams I ever worked with was very eclectic—everyone was different. If you were an outsider looking at our team, it probably didn't make much sense. We had athletes, artists, musicians, talkers, introverts, a lawyer, a mom, and even a few high-schoolers. It sounds like an odd mix, doesn't it? But that mix was the perfect staff for a summer camp. We were very effective. Why? Because we all brought different gifts and abilities to the table with a common mission: to reach all the different kids who were coming to the camp. To do this, we needed all kinds of people.

Teams Increase Volunteer Retention

When people serve by themselves, it could be easy for them to quit and move on to something else if they feel isolated or don't have that all-important interaction with their teammates. Others function well on their own. But most tend to want to be part of a group.

It's inevitable that at some point as a volunteer you will feel overwhelmed or want to give up, but that is where your team can help you. Talk with them, share your struggles, your frustrations, your concerns. Team members remind you, by word and deed, that you aren't alone, that you can do it together. They will support you. Strong teams have members who are not only committed to the cause, they are committed to each other. Like glue, they stick together—and stick to it.

Teams Solve Problems

In any ministry, large or small, there will be problems. That's reality, so don't be surprised when plans go awry or when issues come up among team members. They can be good problems, like outgrowing your meeting room. But there also are matters such as having to talk with a difficult parent whom no one can seem to please. And then there is everything in between. You will find that even with the best leader and the best people serving, you will need creative solutions for the problems you encounter. As a team, you can brainstorm. Become sounding boards for one another, and you will learn to handle situations better.

Teams Are Better at Finding Replacements

As you serve and volunteer, you should always be thinking about replacements. In the first part of this chapter, Alexa almost missed that as she thought about the high-school ministry she was leaving. She nearly overlooked the fact that having Mr. Collins on the team meant that the ministry could continue after she left.

It's hard to step to one side when you've been with a ministry for a while and you know that you've been doing God's work. And we all lean toward running things the way we think is best.

One of the side effects of volunteering is that it can make us feel good about ourselves. That's not bad, but we need to be able to step back and realize we are a part of something greater and that the ministry is not about us or about what we think is best. Sometimes the most loving and insightful thing we can do is to take the selfless, sacrificial step of mentoring and encouraging others to join and eventually take our place. We want others to be part of spreading the life-changing message of Jesus Christ. And we should rejoice when that happens. Those you train will be ready to step in when you, for whatever reason, need to move on. The goal should be the continuation and multiplication of the ministry.

Ten Hints for Leading Teams

What do you need as a volunteer on a team? How can you prepare for success? Below are a few things to think about when you are working with your group. If you are leading other volunteers, you'll want to keep these in mind. Talk with your leader if you feel that any of these are becoming a problem. The goal is not to criticize or blame; it's to develop volunteer teams that are healthy, happy, effective, and attractive to more volunteers.

1. *Have clear expectations.* Uncertainty and ambiguity are the enemies of all volunteers, recruiters, and teams. Leaders should be clear about what is expected. If you don't know what is expected of you in your position as a volunteer, ask.

2. *Know what to do and how to do it.* Every volunteer needs and deserves training. To succeed, each person will need to know

what it takes to successfully execute his or her job. It might be a five-minute explanation with the opportunity for questions, on-the-job preparation, or something else entirely. Some leaders may host a group workshop over several hours or days for more in-depth and comprehensive training. If you are a volunteer and you don't feel like you know what you are doing, ask for some training. You'll want to feel confident and effective in what you do.

3. *Connect your ministry with the larger vision.* Where does your team fit into the overall goals of the church or organization? Sometimes it can be helpful to meet with other teams to see what they are doing. This spreads health and effectiveness and creates a culture of healthy volunteering. Let groups visit and observe each other's ministries. Seeing how others do their volunteer activities is often better than reading, or attending seminars and lectures.

4. *Communicate.* Regular communication to the group and within the group is essential to a healthy, effective, God-honoring volunteer team. It provides occasion to circulate important information and keeps everyone in the know. Communication should be short, frequent, varied, and personal—emails, texts, phone calls, social media, regular group meetings, or a quick coffee. Leaders should welcome questions and comments, and should do their best to reply quickly, whether electronically or in person. If you are a volunteer, do you know where to find out the information you need from your leaders? Do you know how to get in touch with a leader if you have a problem or question? Make sure you find this out, pay attention to what is communicated, and ask if something is not clear.

5. *Celebrate accomplishments.* When goals are met, milestones are passed, or significant things happen, celebrate! Take time as a team to talk about the good things God is doing in the

ministry. Share those moments with your team. Sometimes the wonderful results are missed if someone doesn't stop and point them out. So take a few minutes during your next time together to rejoice in all the good that has happened. And when you hear a story from someone you serve, share it with the rest of the team. Sometimes those who are in behind-the-scenes roles need to hear these encouraging stories to be reminded that what they are doing makes a difference too.

6. *Let others lead.* There are times when the team leader may delegate responsibility. If you are asked to lead, even if you aren't sure whether you can do it, give it a try. The only way to grow is to make the attempt. On a healthy team, the leader will let others take charge of different areas, giving helpful feedback as they grow in those areas. When volunteers lead, they gain a stronger sense of ownership and develop new gifts. Small opportunities to lead will also prepare you for greater leadership roles in the church or the organization. With multiple healthy leaders in different areas, teams will perform better. The best leaders share responsibilities and appreciate watching others learn leadership principles.

7. *Make your team a welcome place to be.* Every team creates a distinct culture. One of the dangers, though, is that they sometimes close themselves off to others outside their circle. Nothing will make new people run from your ministry area faster than thinking they really aren't wanted. Don't be a closed community. Aim to be a group that accepts and loves new members. Remember that more people on the team often means a more influential ministry and, ultimately, more people meeting Jesus Christ.

8. *Respect everyone's time.* Nothing makes most volunteers frustrated and annoyed more than wasting their time. It's important for meetings to start and end when expected. As a

volunteer, make sure you aren't contributing to delays or disrupting things by arriving late. Another annoyance is when someone hijacks the discussion or the conversation, focusing on minor topics or personal anecdotes that don't apply. Be sure the conversation isn't all about you, and honor the agenda that your leaders have set. Whether you are a volunteer or a volunteer leader, remember that everyone's time is valuable.

9. *Have parties!* Ministries can sometimes lose their energy when they don't encourage relationships apart from the work before them. So remember to have fun together regularly. Team members who know each other and care about each other will get better results, and they will further enjoy what they are doing. Do your part to help foster an atmosphere in which spending time laughing together, sharing each other's lives, and enjoying each other's company is an essential part of your group's ministry. Don't be afraid to hang out with other volunteers outside the formal ministry times. Have them over to your home, see a movie together, and develop friendships that go beyond the time you spend volunteering.

10. *Say thank you.* When you notice someone on your team "going beyond the call of duty" or finishing a challenging project, express your thanks and regard for their efforts. If you are a leader of volunteers, this is especially important to remember. Use your words and actions to thank those with whom you serve. Set aside time to write notes and send emails and texts of encouragement. Become a master at noticing all the great things the people on your team do and acknowledging them, both privately and publicly.

Keep these hints in mind as you volunteer and serve, and you will develop a ministry team with healthy and happy volunteers, one that attracts new volunteers to your group.

Questions for Reflection and Discussion

1. Think about the team you serve on or hope to serve on. From what you know, are there any particular gifts, skill sets, or talents missing on your team, and do you know anyone who could be recruited to fill those roles?

   _____

2. What do you think is the most important thing for a team to do to create a healthy community for serving together?

CHAPTER 4

Storytelling

YOURS, MINE, HIS

As a little girl growing up on a farm, I had many friends. There was Sally the salamander, Pepper the mutt dog, Will the goldfish, Lucy the collie, Lovey the schnauzer, and Missy the Siamese cat—to name just a few. As I added new friends, there was always space for them.

Now that I'm older, I look back at that time and realize it helped to foster my love of animals. But if I'm honest, it was really my mother's influence that started my fascination. My mom was always quick to point out a new animal and discover a new way for us to learn about it, whether we were visiting the zoo, watching TV, or just wandering around the farm.

I remember one night I was watching a new television program that Mom had found for me. Loud noises emerged from our TV as animals ran across the open land in Yellowstone National Park. It was all pretty amazing for a little girl who loved animals. Watching the show, I was hooked, and I was sure that Yellowstone National Park was the most wonderful animal place in the whole world.

It was another ten years before I got to visit Yellowstone, but eventually I made it. Before arriving, I already had a wonderful picture of the place in my mind. The TV show had given me a vision of a place where animals roamed free. Because that story was told with beauty and majesty, it stirred up passion in me and gave me a yearning to see it for myself.

That's what stories do. They evoke life in us, new desires and yearnings that take us outside of ourselves. Maybe you've heard a story that has made you want to save the world. Or you've seen a movie or read a book and felt something so deeply that tears came to your eyes. Stories have power. Jesus used stories to get his teaching about God and God's kingdom across to people. Jesus knew that he could state a truth, but it might not resonate in the hearts of those listening. So more often than not, he created word pictures—stories and parables—so people could clearly understand the truth in their hearts and minds.

Do you remember the first time you read the parable of the prodigal son? What kind of emotions did you feel as you imagined the story of the Good Samaritan? As noted previously, Jesus, the master storyteller, understood that stories engage people, and that's why he used them with his followers. By teaching them through stories, he prepared them to share the greatest story of all—the story of his life, death, and resurrection.

So how can you use stories in your ministry area as a volunteer? There is a great deal we can learn from the method Jesus used.

Stories Bring Alignment

"What color should we paint the entryway of the church building?"

"Blue!"

"No! It has to be gray!"

"Yellow is such an inviting color! Don't you want us to look like a friendly church?"

Unfortunately, it doesn't take much to start a disagreement, even in church. It can happen in a matter of minutes over something as simple as a can of paint. That is why a volunteer group needs to learn to think in alignment.

One of the best ways to achieve alignment is by sharing and utilizing stories. Stories can move a team forward in the direction it needs to go. If your team leader senses a group might be starting to splinter, he or she is probably thinking about a story to get all of you back on the same page. It might be a reminder of the little boy who came to faith a few weeks ago, or the single mom the church has been praying for who opened up and began to talk after one of you brought a meal to her home. You also might have your own anecdote that will provide a positive context for a disagreement or division.

As a volunteer, practice telling stories. Remind each other of your true purpose, the goal you are all working toward. Be like Jesus, who constantly used stories to keep his disciples moving in the same direction.

Keep Going in the Same Direction

The vision had been cast. Our group of volunteers shared a common dream—to build up the young adults in our church so they were passionate about reaching the next generation. Our volunteers were invited to do two things. First, to pray that God would use our small group to reach this generation. And second, to pray that we'd be blessed with opportunities to make new friends, and to reach out to the young adults in our area in their places of work and in the community. It was exciting for us to be praying together, asking God to do something beyond what we could do. The volunteers could picture what it would look like to see those they loved coming to faith in Jesus and having their lives transformed.

Several months had passed since the vision had first been shared, and the initial excitement had dwindled. The demands of work, school, sports activities, and the exhaustion of the daily routines of life had distracted us from our focus.

And then Mark shared a story. He talked about what was happening in his small group. The group was filled with young men who were on the verge of coming to know Christ. Some had even made recent commitments. One of the young men in the group named Nick had heard about the vision to reach the young adults in our community several months earlier, but he had never talked about it much. Then one night at their small group meeting, Nick spoke up. "I can really see the vision, and I have been convicted that so many other young people don't know Jesus. So I invited four of my friends to church this week." Mark, the small-group leader, was excited to witness Nick's continued growth and to meet several of his friends. As Mark shared the story of how God was working in his group with the other small-group leaders, there were some tears, and we all sensed a renewed motivation growing among the volunteer leaders. The vision was becoming a reality.

As a volunteer, don't be shy about sharing examples of how God is working in the things you do. Even if it doesn't seem like a big deal, you never know how God will use your story to inspire others. Don't let your experiences and your stories be wasted. They are just what other volunteers may need in a moment of exhaustion or discouragement. Not only do they inspire others to keep going, these stories attract others to get involved.

But I'm Not a Storyteller!

Maybe you think you aren't very good at telling stories. Memorable anecdotes surround us, but we often miss them. We just need to pay attention and keep our eyes open. We get busy with our tasks and stop seeing the beauty and the power in what is happening right in front of us. So learn to pay attention. Here are a few suggestions that might help.

- Listen to the stories of those you serve. Often, those in your area of ministry—young and old and in between—have things they want to talk about, prayer needs, and struggles. Take the time to listen to them. Some of the stories you share may not be about you, but they are about the people to whom you are ministering. (When you share a story that might have sensitive details, be sure you get permission from the person first.)
- Your story doesn't need to be long or complicated. Some are about steps in the right direction, and they don't necessarily end with someone professing Christ or a sick person being miraculously healed. Sometimes the ordinary stories of faithful ministry, the small things that people do over time, can have the greatest impact.
- It sounds simple, but there are those who might be happy to share their story if someone simply asked them. Ask your class or small group, "What have you seen God do in your life recently?"
- If you have a good memory, you might consider becoming a story collector, someone who seeks out positive, faith-building stories to share with others.

We've all seen movies or read novels that have captured our minds and our hearts. There is an art to telling a story well. And doing it well is the difference between someone paying attention and wanting more—or tuning out. Make it your goal to get better at telling stories, and think about these guidelines.

- Keep the story simple. If it's too long or complicated, people will stop listening. Fit the anecdote to the audience's age, interests, and attention span.
- Set the stage for those listening. Don't just relate facts or information. Try to paint a picture of the setting to help people engage with what you are saying with understanding and insight. Your audience will be keyed in, anticipating where the story is going.
- Use words people can understand. Don't forget that those who haven't been part of a church may feel sidelined by phrases Christians are used to hearing. Know the experiences and context of your audience. Some people stop listening because they aren't familiar with the terminology, not because they aren't interested.

Let stories ricochet throughout your church, encouraging you as a volunteer and reminding others in your church about the rewards, both earthly and heavenly, of volunteering. Allow them to attract others to your church and to your ministry area. Stories are one of the most powerful tools you have to expand the vision, encourage others, and draw in new volunteers.

Questions for Reflection and Discussion

1. Who is the best storyteller on your team? How can you help that person to get more stories shared?

_____

2. Who might be a good story collector on your volunteer team? Someone organized and diligent would be a top candidate.

_____

3. Where are some places to post stories about a volunteer's experiences (first with your own team, then with other volunteers, as well as the whole congregation)?

CHAPTER 5

Recruiting

EVERYBODY CAN DO IT!

I live in Minnesota, and that means one thing. *Cold* winters. Really cold. Minnesotans don't let the weather stop them from living; it just requires extra clothing. When I first moved to Minnesota, I was amazed by the games the native Minnesotans played out in the cold, particularly broomball. For those who have never played broomball, it is hockey without skates. Oh, and instead of a hockey stick, you use a broom all wrapped up with tape at the bottom to hit a small ball, not a puck, into a net. Oh, and one more thing—did I mention there are no helmets?

At our church we were wondering how we could attract young adults who don't know Jesus. One of our underutilized resources is a place called Goose Poop Pond (clearly having gotten its name from the ones that spend most of their time there). It's the run-off pond for the church campus, and we figured it would make an excellent broomball rink when it froze. An idea worth pursuing, I thought, so I gathered a few volunteers to share the vision. We had a great meeting—all three of us! At the end of the meeting, my volunteers looked at me. "This is a great idea," they said, "but where are you going to find the other volunteers?"

Has that happened to you? The big idea leader sweet talks you into a meeting and expresses the big idea with lots of enthusiasm. You want to be involved, but you don't want to go it alone.

At this point, many volunteers decide that it's easier to sit back and let the staff member or pastor find more people for the volunteer team. But let me share a new perspective with you. The reality is that your team is *most likely* to grow if you, the volunteer, join in the effort. This is one of the primary ways volunteers serve the ministry they love.

Why Should *Everyone* Do the Recruiting?

More people recruiting will lead to more volunteers. You, as a volunteer, know different people than the staff or the leader of your ministry. The more connections you can make means there are more possible volunteers to join the team. I have a coworker who always uses Legos to illustrate this. We each have connecting points like the top of a Lego. The more Legos you have, the more connecting points you have with more people.

In addition, different people have different kinds of influence. Not every person will respond to a leader casting a vision or a direct request to help out. Different personalities and differing approaches are needed to make the case. Someone may say yes to you but might say no to another person because of the way they are asked and who is doing the asking.

I know a team that was brainstorming about individuals to join their ministry group. When Janna's name came up, everyone agreed instantly that she was the perfect fit for the position. All the names, including Janna's, were divided up to make contacting them more manageable. A week later, the team gathered again to update each other on their week of volunteer recruitment. Mike said that he had talked with Janna, and she said to him that she just wasn't sure. Amanda, who was sitting across the room, quickly spoke up. "I guess I should have asked her since I know her the best. Let me give it a try." Amanda found Janna later that week at church and mentioned that she knew Mike had talked to her about joining the team. Amanda talked about the volunteer role, but she also shared *why* she thought Janna would be a good fit, knowing her strengths. At the end of their fifteen-minute conversation, Janna looked at Amanda and said, "Well you've clearly thought through why I'd be a good person to add to the team. I guess I can't say no! Sure. I'll do it!"

We all know different people in different ways. If you are thinking about joining a volunteer team, who are you more likely to say yes to? Would you say yes to someone who knows you, your gifts, talents, and abilities, or someone who merely knows your name? Like most of us, you'll say yes to the person who knows you well; you trust her and you trust she wouldn't ask you to do something you wouldn't enjoy or that you wouldn't do well.

It's also encouraging to know that you aren't the only one responsible for recruiting. It can be overwhelming to do this all by yourself. It's tiring and, at times, discouraging. One of our volunteers, a man named Jacob, was sitting on the lobby couch at church with his head in his hands. Carmen cheerfully came walking around the corner, saw his woeful expression, and stopped to talk. "Looks like you've got a problem!" she said to him.

Jacob shook his head and forced a chuckle. "Yes, I need about twenty volunteers to pull off this outreach event, and I have five." Carmen plopped down on the couch by him and smiled, "Well, it sounds like you need a little help. Why don't I help you come up with those volunteers?" Jacob felt his heart lift at her words. He went from feeling overwhelmed to believing this just possibly could be done. Working together, Jacob and Carmen prayed and came up with names until the team was complete.

When we try to recruit on our own, it's easy to be blown away by the enormity of the task. Having at least one other person join with you in the effort takes it from the realm of daunting to achievable. Who doesn't appreciate a partner in these endeavors?

As you serve with other volunteers, agree that you will make the work of recruiting others a team project. More people recruiting means more people serving. And this means more ministry happening and more people meeting Jesus. Isn't that what it's all about?

When our broomball ministry finally launched, we had two hundred people playing. I can assure you that it took more than those first two volunteers to pull it off. It took dozens to facilitate sign-ups, build the rink, organize the food, and set up the playing schedule. The most exciting part of the process was seeing all of the volunteers find their purpose and realize they were needed to do their part to reach more young adults for Jesus Christ.

Getting Started

So what can you as a volunteer do to recruit others? Make sure to pray with your fellow volunteer team members when you see the need for additional help, whether in your own area or elsewhere. Remember what it was like when you started out as a new volunteer in the ministry. Discuss with your group what your fears were as you began your place in the ministry, and talk about what captivated you and brought you to the team.

Make a list of the people you know who are potential candidates for this role. Should you email, call, or have coffee in person? God ultimately does the recruiting, and you are just asking on his behalf. Encourage one another when multiple people say no. God is bigger than those negative responses. Don't give up!

Make sure you have a clear understanding of the job you are recruiting someone to do. When you share the opportunity, be ready for his or her questions. Most volunteers want to know more than just the specific responsibility. Most important is the overall vision of the particular ministry area. They of course will need details like times, frequency, meetings they need to attend, etc. If you aren't sure, ask your leader.

There is nothing better than having a group of people recruiting and asking others to join the team. People feel important and special when they are invited to be a part of a ministry, so make it personal whenever you can. But don't neglect other great ways to get the word out to new people for your area of ministry. Use weekly communication at your church as well as the website and social networking sites to get the word out. Consider making a video to share with others. You might ask the pastor to include a mention of the opportunity during the service, or suggest making an announcement about the ministry opportunity.

Invite your possible recruit to visit your ministry area, and make sure it is organized so the visit is positive. Prospective volunteers might want to talk with other volunteers about the ministry in which they might serve.

Recruiting is a big part of every volunteer program. As a volunteer, you can embrace the role of recruiting others. It's not simply the responsibility of the staff, the pastors, or the team leader to find others to help. If we are honest, we know recruiting takes effort and courage, but if you want to see your ministry area grow and multiply, it will take more people, so pray, be brave, and ask. Go after those other possible team members. You can do it!

Questions for Reflection and Discussion

1. When you think of recruiting other volunteers, do you feel excited or nervous? Have you ever done it before? How did it go for you?

   _____

2. Think of examples from your volunteer experience—or from others you've heard about—that you could share with a possible recruit. Tell the story to a friend, family member, or another volunteer for some confidence-building practice.

   _____

3. What new ideas or initiatives would you like to see happen in your area of ministry? Where do you see a need for a new volunteer?

   _____

4. Write down some steps you can take this week to begin recruiting new people to your area.

CHAPTER 6

Volunteers Get Paid??

Caleb sat on his tiny blue chair, feet dangling above a cracked tile floor that desperately needed updating. He looked around at his four friends. All five of them sat laughing and talking with coloring sheets of Noah and the Ark and a worn box of crayons on the little old table in front of them.

To a five-year-old boy, Wilma, Caleb's Sunday-school teacher, looked like she was a hundred years old. Whatever her age, Caleb knew that she was there each Sunday to teach him in that small church basement. She was always there. She never missed a Sunday.

Now much older and soon to become a pastor at a church, Caleb was asked to talk about his decision to become a pastor. He thought back to his experiences growing up in that small church with the cracked tile floor. Tears welled up in his eyes as he remembered Wilma's patient and smiling face. He talked about how he had struggled with school, what an effort it had been to read and write, and how wonderful it had been to go to Sunday school and to have a teacher who handed him a sticker when he got only half the verse right. He found encouragement to push ahead, and he learned that he was okay even with his inadequacies. He knew that his teacher, Wilma, believed in him and wouldn't give up on him. And it was just what he needed. Someone besides his parents believed in him and loved him.

Looking back on those early years in that small church, what struck Caleb most was not the lessons or the specific Bible stories. Wilma had not turned him into a little Bible scholar; she had modeled Jesus' character. She saw in him what he couldn't see in himself. Just like Jesus does.

Wilma's name doesn't show up in the Bible, but she is one of the great heroes in the story of the kingdom to come. She gave herself every week to a group of small children so they could experience who Jesus is, repeatedly recounting to them his teachings. She never won any awards for her service, but she continued to serve year after year.

When No One Notices

As a volunteer, there may be weeks, months, or sadly, even years that go by without a thank-you. There won't be a bouquet of flowers sent to your house for the fifty diapers you changed that year in the nursery. And you may not get a thank-you note for the four hours every other week you spent mowing the church lawn last summer. That wayward teenage boy from youth group whom you drove all the way across town to get released from jail will probably not stop to thank you for caring when his parents didn't.

Hopefully you *will* hear the words thank you at least some of the time. But even so, there will be times when you will want to throw your hands up in the air in discouragement or disgust. But don't. You need to realize that there is more than one reward and that there is a thank you yet to come, one that matters more than any other. Think bigger, think greater. Think Matthew 25:40: "Whatever you did for one of the least of these brothers of mine, you did for me." This is a verse all volunteers should have burned into their minds. When we volunteer, while it is nice to hear a thank you, we aren't serving for that. We serve for God, and we do it so others find out about him. Caleb never said the words "thank you" to Wilma, but he talks about her now and freely shares the impact she had on his life. Though she is no longer alive, she is one of the reasons he is a pastor today.

Many times we will never know how we have impacted someone's faith journey until we meet them again in heaven. But that doesn't mean we should opt out of serving. It means we keep our perspective focused on the long view, remembering the real reason why we do what we do. Sure, appreciation is nice, and we should all look for ways to express it to each other. But don't serve for the applause of others. Don't volunteer for the pat on the back. That's not why we volunteer.

Luke 17:11–19 relates the story of Jesus on his way to Jerusalem. He passes through a village and comes across ten men who had leprosy. Having pity on these men, he heals them and tells them to go show themselves to the priests. They all leave, but only one of them returns to Jesus to express his gratitude: "when he saw he was healed, [he] came back, praising God in a loud voice. He threw himself at Jesus' feet and thanked him — and he was a Samaritan."

Of the ten, only one of the healed lepers came back to say thank you. And the one who came was the least likely to do so, the one readers would have not expected. There will be times when we are doing what God has called us to do, but we don't get the reaction that we expect. Remember that even Jesus experienced this. It's not about us, it's not about the reward we get here and now; it's about our true reward that awaits us in the life to come. We have been called to remain faithful and keep the truth in the forefront of our minds, whether or not we hear the words "thank you."

Still ... You *Can* Say Thank You

If you can relate to what I've just shared and have been tempted toward bitterness or frustration because of a lack of appreciation for what you've done, let me give you one suggestion. Don't make the same mistake. Be the one who *does* say thank you. Be the champion in your church for making it the place where the words "thank you" are endlessly exchanged. Be the one to step up and talk with your church leaders about expressing thanks frequently and often! Be a part of putting together a yearly plan for what this could look like. Remember, if it's not on the calendar or the to-do list, it can—and likely will be—overlooked.

- Plan a party just to thank the volunteers. It doesn't have to be big or cost a lot, just special.
- Send one weekly thank-you note to a volunteer in the church and try to cover everyone by the end of the year. Make it personal, not a ritual.
- Suggest that leaders make a habit of walking around church when things are happening. Notice what volunteers are doing and say, "Thank you for _____."
- Ask volunteers for their prayer requests, and then remember to follow up and ask how things are going.
- Highlight a volunteer story in the weekly communication or have a volunteer-of- the-week spotlight.

- Ask the children and students in your church to write why they appreciate the volunteers in the church; it will speak to hearts instantly.

None of these things have to be elaborate; they just need to be intentional. You'd be surprised by the difference a small note or a verbal thank-you will make in your church culture. On the other hand, remember that you may never hear a thank-you, but keep your perspective on the bigger picture. If you don't think yours is a thanking church, be the volunteer who changes that. (By the way, that is a great volunteer role—the ministry of thanking others.)

Questions for Reflection and Discussion

1. Who are the people around you who need the encouragement of a thank-you?

   _____

2. What are some ways you could thank other volunteer or team leaders? (They can use a word of appreciation too!)

CHAPTER 7

The Benefits Package

We've looked at some reasons why people should volunteer and seen that, ultimately, it's because God calls us to volunteer. What better reason might you find? To encourage you even further, here are some additional benefits to giving your time and resources to serving others.

Health Benefits

Did you know there are both physical and emotional health benefits when you offer yourself to help others? When you show up to volunteer, you don't merely make a difference in others' lives. You will begin to see differences in your own. You might even begin to feel healthier and less stressed. Just spend some time googling "health benefits with volunteering" and you'll see what I'm talking about. Take a look at a few of the studies and their findings.

The United Health Group, headquartered in Minnetonka, Minnesota, is a large company that focuses on health-care coverage and benefits services. As a business, they feel it is important to promote volunteering among their employees. They commissioned some research on the benefits of volunteering so they could share the results with their employees.[2] They conducted a national survey in 2013 on volunteering among 3,351 adults. Here are some statistics that emerged:

- 76 percent of people who volunteered in the last twelve months say that volunteering has made them feel healthier.
- 78 percent of people who volunteered in the last twelve months say that volunteering lowers their stress.
- 94 percent of people who volunteered in the last twelve months say that volunteering improves their mood.

This and other studies tell us that volunteering is good for you. Volunteers have better personal scores than nonvolunteers on nine well-established measures of emotional well-being, including personal independence, capacity for rich interpersonal relationships, and overall satisfaction with life. Volunteering also has been shown to improve a person's attitude and build self-esteem.

Fascinating, isn't it? But wait, there is more. Let's look at what the US Census Bureau and the Centers for Disease Control found when looking at the United States. They determined that "states with a high volunteer rate also have lower rates of mortality and incidences of heart disease. When comparing states, a general trend shows that health problems are more prevalent in states where volunteer rates are lowest."[3] Living longer? A decreased risk for heart disease? That sounds pretty good to me!

The London School of Economics also took a look at how volunteering affects you—not only the health benefits but your overall happiness. When researchers examined the relationship between volunteering and measures of happiness in a large group of American adults, they found that the more people volunteered, the happier they were. Published results of their study in *Social Science and Medicine* show that compared with people who never volunteered, the odds of being "very happy" rose

7 percent among those who volunteer monthly and 12 percent for people who volunteer every two to four weeks. And among weekly volunteers, 16 percent felt very happy, a hike in happiness that is comparable to having an income of $75,000–$100,000 versus $20,000, say the researchers. They also found that what you do as a volunteer makes a difference. Giving time to religious organizations had the greatest impact overall on a person's level of happiness.[4]

Keep in mind that we're not talking about just statistics here. These are real people. Real lives. Consider two men, both well into their eighties. Both had lost their wives to cancer. One of them had even buried an adult child. As they were interviewed about their lives and responded to questions about their relationship with Jesus and the volunteer work they did, they smiled, laughed, and talked about living with passion. In all the advice they shared, something clearly stuck out. Their lives had meaning because they knew Jesus Christ and they were committed to serving him. Both of these men had continued to serve even in their later years.

One of them was volunteering with a younger-adults church group. He would show up at their weekly meeting and always listened carefully to the young people share about their lives, and he would pray for them. The other man was "giving back" from his assisted-living center, taking time to meet with, pray for, and share from his years of experience with young pastors. These two men could have sat around thinking about their losses in life, growing bitter because of life's circumstances. Instead, they chose to live their lives in a way that brought glory to God. They were still giving of themselves and investing in others, knowing that they did have something to offer. It was a gift to those they served, but it also brought life and health to themselves.

There are many signs that point to the benefits of volunteering. If you find yourself not feeling well, trapped in an emotional downturn, or if you simply want to take a new initiative with your health, it might be time to find a volunteer role. The results are real, and it may even lead to happier days and a longer life.

Professional Benefits

In addition to the health benefits, volunteering can help you in your professional growth as well. Volunteering for Sunday school taught a young woman named Sarah how to better facilitate a classroom when she became a teacher. Volunteering at camp as the activities director taught Ryan how to effectively lead large group meetings at his business, keeping others motivated and engaged. Volunteering weekly at church to update the visitor contact information allowed Meg to practice the computer skills she needed to land her job as an administrative assistant at the local college.

Volunteering can help you develop and maximize your skill set. Serving as a volunteer provides you with the opportunity to learn and try new things. It allows you to find out what you do well and enjoy, and it might even lead you down a new career path.

Jackie stood up and shook the hand offered to her. She thanked the interviewer for the opportunity, breathed a sigh of relief, and walked out the front door. She felt confident in the answers that she had given to each question. She was thankful for the many relevant examples she'd been able to provide from the various volunteer roles she had held over the last several years. The last hour had been a great opportunity for her to tell about examples of team building, responses to difficult situations, persistence in the midst of challenge, and effective networking. Jackie's time volunteering at church not only had given her many spiritual and personal benefits but also had given her professional confidence and skills.

Volunteering is about giving yourself to honor God and serve others, but we shouldn't be surprised to learn that it also provides something in return. If you are in need of professional experience, personal growth, and opportunities for building self-confidence, find a volunteer role. You too could have an experience similar to Jackie's.

Educational Benefits

Along with health and professional benefits, there is also the opportunity to learn new things. Michelle, Kristina, and Heidi found this out when they signed up to serve on a cross-cultural mission trip. The three girls had finally managed to fall asleep in the double bed they would be sharing for the next several nights. It wasn't just the lack of personal space they were adjusting to but also the fact that the house they were staying in was on stilts above the ocean. That night they were startled awake by the calls of their host. She was waving her arms and shouting to them in a language they could not understand, but it was not long before her meaning became clear. Rain began trickling through the roof and onto the three of them.

Early the next morning as the girls hung up their wet bedding, they reflected on all the unique experiences the trip had provided. Showering at the well, playing the local favorite sport, and catching and preparing the meal for the evening were only a few. The girls had volunteered their time to serve a group of individuals living on the island, and the next two weeks passed swiftly. Soon the girls were packing their bags to go home. They had come to the island to help the people there, but what they were given in return was astonishing. They had learned about a new culture, met new people, and found out a lot about themselves as well.

When you volunteer, whether overseas or down the street from your house, you are sure to learn some new things. You will discover what is going on in your community. You will learn about how others live. You will learn about yourself and how you respond to new situations, how you tackle problems, and how you work with different kinds of people and personalities. If you feel out of touch or don't know what is going on in your community or the world around you, become a volunteer. It's an intentional way to be a lifelong learner.

Questions for Reflection and Discussion

1. What are some of the benefits you'd like to gain from volunteering? Are there any others that come to mind, besides the ones mentioned in this chapter?

   _____

2. How have you seen others benefit from volunteering? What difference did it make in their lives?

CHAPTER 8

Avoiding Burnout

Crosby's first year of volunteering with the college students was fantastic. He sincerely loved spending time with them and signed up for the next year without hesitation. Now, three months into year two, it was another story. Crosby was exhausted. It wasn't just the extra hour a week that he spent driving in rush-hour traffic to his volunteer commitment. He found that the exhaustion was setting in *during* that extra hour. He spent the time mulling over all the issues he was dealing with in his life.

Crosby had a family member battling with health issues. At his daytime job, he was struggling with difficult coworkers and had numerous deadlines hanging over his head. A failed relationship with a girl he had dreamed of a future with had ended in tears and hurt feelings. It all felt like too much. The thought of showing up again for the weekly meetings and trying to focus on leading his small group was overwhelming.

Over the next few months, Crosby did nothing to change his situation. He didn't talk to anyone about what was happening in his life. Things continued to pile up. He had trouble managing his daily life and his relationships, and soon the other volunteer leaders began to notice that Crosby was coming in late to their leader meetings. Then he stopped showing up altogether. He screened out phone calls from the other leaders. They sent notes and emails to him, and even though he felt guilty about it, he didn't reply. Crosby never officially quit; he just disappeared.

What leads to burnout? Why does a volunteer just disappear one day? Sometimes the position feels like too much and volunteers aren't sure what to do. Or life outside of the volunteer role becomes unmanageable. Health issues, workload, school and family commitments—all kinds of issues can get in the way. And sometimes it's just a bad fit between the volunteer and the position, and the constant stress of serving in a bad fit feels like dread instead of feeling like a sweet spot.

Many different things can cause burnout, but what can you do to avoid it? How do you overcome the difficulties and enjoy serving again?

Talk to Someone

If you feel like you are on the verge of burnout, say something to someone as soon as you've identified it. If you ignore it or try to keep going by sheer willpower and don't come clean about how you are feeling, it's only going to get worse.

Crosby's biggest mistake was that he didn't say anything to anybody. Instead of his problems going away, he grew even more frustrated and felt alone with his struggles. Things went from bad to worse. When you feel that hint of burnout, it's time to talk with someone. Let your leader and those you volunteer with know what is going on so they are aware, can pray for you, and give some counsel on dealing with it.

Your fellow volunteers will be glad to support you in the hard things that are going on in your life. It might be as simple as being overwhelmed with your volunteer role and finding that you need a hand from another volunteer. That is a problem that can be solved. Or it might be that you need someone to help you with your day-to-day life so you can still be part of the volunteer team. A few hours of help with the yard work or even just a chance to talk with someone might be just the answer to the shortage of time you've had, would alleviate stress, and keep you on the team. You don't want to be the volunteer who just disappears, so make sure you speak up and ask for help. If the issue turns out to be bigger than your team leader or other members can address, they will direct you to someone more experienced to give some counsel.

Find a New Role or Take a Break

Becca called to inform me that she'd be done volunteering soon. At first, I was sad and surprised. She was one of the best volunteers we had. As we talked, I asked how things were going in her life, and she explained that she had a few things coming up in the next six months at work and would be out of town a lot. The thought of managing all that as well as her volunteer role seemed overwhelming to her. I listened carefully and then asked, "Becca, would you still like to be on the volunteer team if you could just take a little sabbatical or if I could find you another role that wouldn't be so large?" Silence, then I heard a couple of sobs.

"Really?" she finally was able to say. "It would work for me to stay on, even if it's not exactly what I signed up for?"

I said, "Sure!" Becca was thrilled and so was I.

Before you think of quitting because of difficult situations, talk with your leader about your options. In some circumstances, it might be best to end your time as a volunteer. But in other circumstances, you may just need a little time off, or maybe you can fill another volunteer role that isn't so daunting at the moment. The key to not burning out may be as simple as some creative problem solving with your leader.

Finding the Right Fit

As we discussed in an earlier chapter, it's important to remember that your fit with a ministry and a role really do matter. Burnout will happen if you are in the wrong role and your volunteering experience goes from life-giving to life-consuming. If it's not the right fit, don't just give up. Tell one of the leaders at church and let your leader help you find your place. Yes, the the other volunteers in your ministry area will be sad to see you go, but they'd rather have you as a happy volunteer than not volunteering at all.

Questions for Reflection and Discussion

1. Have you ever experienced burnout? If so, what happened? What did you do when you knew you were burned out? How did it end?

   _____

2. What are some of the warning signs of burnout? What things in your life right now could be triggers for burnout?

   _____

3. What are some steps you can take this week to change direction and avoid burning out as a volunteer?

CHAPTER 9

Prayer Matters

Brodie and Aimee were asked by a highly respected friend to help volunteer for an event, and they immediately said yes. But after sending an email confirming their involvement, Aimee looked at Brodie and asked an important question: "Will we be good at this?" They had signed up to take two adults with special needs Christmas shopping. Brodie and Aimee had clocked hundreds of volunteer hours in many different ministries, but they had never done anything like this. To say they weren't nervous would be a falsehood. What if they made a mistake? What if the individuals didn't like them? What if the two couldn't properly supervise them? The what-ifs continued playing in their minds over the next week.

A few weeks later on a cold December evening, they pulled into the mall to begin their assignment. As they were about to hop out of the SUV, Brodie suggested, "Let's pray about the night. I know we're both really nervous about this." So they prayed. They asked the Lord to help them do well with this new activity and to use them to serve the two people they were paired with for the evening.

They joined the group inside the mall, checked in, and soon were partnered with Monica and Kyle. The two young adults quickly announced to them the amount of money they had and exactly what they needed for perfect gifts to give their friends and family. As the four walked from store to store in search of graphic tees and apple-scented soaps, both Brodie and Aimee found that their anxiety had been replaced with peace and joy. They listened to Monica and Kyle talk about love interests, their families, and some of the challenges they faced.

Soon the night was almost over. Brodie and Aimee stood smiling as Monica and Kyle ran back to their large group to display all the wonderful gifts they had found. Aimee and Brodie said goodbye to their new friends and thanked Monica and Kyle for a wonderful evening of Christmas shopping.

As Aimee and Brodie made their way through the snowy parking lot to their car, Brodie noticed Aimee brushing tears from her eyes. "It's just so amazing," she said in a choked voice. "I was so nervous about doing and saying the right things. But all I felt tonight was joy in serving."

Brodie agreed and added, "Lifting up our evening in prayer truly reminded me of what is important and why we were doing this in the first place. God really used this opportunity to teach us to trust him." They returned home with hearts full of thanksgiving and wonder that God was able to use them in this new way.

Start and End with Prayer

Whether you are a veteran volunteer or you are new to the role like Brodie and Aimee, make sure you pray. Giving everything over to God—fears and uncertainties, as well as the anticipation and joy—and letting him lead the way is always best. Brodie and Aimee felt apprehensive about their new volunteer role, and they did exactly what the Bible calls for. Philippians 4:6 tells us, "Do not be anxious about anything, but in everything, by prayer and petition, with thanksgiving, present your requests to God."

God cares. He cares about the big things and the small things of our lives, so share them with him before you head into your volunteer time. First Thessalonians 5:16–18 says, "Be joyful always; pray continually; give thanks in all circumstances, for this is God's will for you in Christ Jesus." Did you hear that? Pray continually. So whether you are anxious, nervous, excited, or even if you are feeling fine, dedicate time to pray for the work that you are involved in and the ones you will serve. Let the ultimate leader guide you as you serve others for his glory. Pray.

It's Not About Us

Kate put the finishing touches on the backdrop she had painted for the children's ministry drama for Sunday. She had spent hours drawing, choosing the right colors, and creating just the right set for the Easter drama. Preston, another volunteer, stopped by to admire her work. "It looks great," he said. "Too bad this is just for one morning. We'll be painting over it next week." He probably thought it was a compliment, but Kate felt her face start to redden in frustration. She had known her painting would not be on display for weeks, but Preston's offhand attitude made her feel that her talent wasn't really appreciated.

That night at home, Kate had time to consider Preston's words and her feelings. Before she went to bed, she prayed that God would take away her anger and remind her of what was truly important. That Sunday, as she watched the drama team depict the miraculous events of Easter morning, she forgot about her hours of painting and was again amazed by the message of the story. She was grateful that her creativity and skill had been used in some way to help share a most important message. That time in prayer had reminded her that she was there not to get praise or recognition but to use what God had given her to serve others, even if it would be painted over soon.

When we pray, we are reminding ourselves of who is in charge of the ministry. It's not us, and if we forget to hand our ministry and volunteer role over to God, we are at risk of thinking our ministry area is about what we can do on our own. Prayer underscores the fact that our ministry is for God, about God, and because of God.

Prayer Reminds Us: God Is Powerful

I remember a missions trip to Asia, praying over a woman and seeing immediate changes in her life. I was overcome by the evidence of God's power. I had known in my head that God is powerful, but praying and seeing God answer prayer immediately was breathtaking. As I lay in bed that night in a foreign country, I was frustrated with my lack of faith. I had known for a long time that God is powerful, so why didn't I call on him more often? Knowing that he is capable of great things, why didn't I reach out to him for everything, both the small details and the larger challenges?

God is powerful; we must never forget this. A friend of mine often compares prayer to plugging a lamp into an electrical outlet. Plugging in allows the power to come through the cord and fills the room with light. I'm struck by this every time I think of it: we must plug into the real power source, the power that comes from God.

If you want to see your volunteering and service transformed, you will need to tap into the kind of power that comes only from God. In Matthew 21:21 – 22, Jesus told his followers, "I tell you the truth, if you have faith and do not doubt, not only can you do what was done to the fig tree, but also you can say to this mountain, 'Go, throw yourself into the sea,' and it will be done. If you believe, you will receive whatever you ask for in prayer."

We Aren't Alone

When we look at Jesus, we see an example of how to do life, and that example involves regular times of prayer. Luke 6:12 tells us about him, "One of those days Jesus went out to a mountainside to pray, and spent the night praying to God." Jesus needed time with his Father to sustain him and provide him with power and strength. I also imagine he needed time communing with him to know that he wasn't alone on the journey. Jesus had his twelve disciples serving with him, but it was only his Father who could truly understand his heart and soul.

Like Jesus, I hope that you have a handful of Jesus' disciples you are walking through life with, but there may be times when only God can comfort you and help you see clearly. It might be when another volunteer hurts you with thoughtless words. It might be when you come face to face with your deepest insecurities. Or it might be that you've seen someone's pain and suffering in a way that seems indescribable. Whatever it may be, prayer helps us keep a true perspective. Time spent praying reminds us that we aren't on our own. We can call on God anytime and in any place.

Prayer Is the Best Gift You Can Give

Alan wouldn't stop praising his former volunteer leader, Chris. Honestly, I was becoming annoyed. I wanted to nicely inform Alan that if he told me one more time about how great Chris was, I'd have to stop talking to him. Alan had become one of my newest acquaintances, and I enjoyed him greatly—except for the endless praising of Chris. I knew Chris, and although I found him to be a nice enough guy, I could not understand why Alan felt the need to go on and on about him. One day I couldn't stop myself from asking, "Alan, what's the deal? Why do you think Chris is so amazing?" Alan looked at me and replied, "Because every time Chris sees me, he stops and prays for me. I'm dying of cancer."

I had no words. I didn't know about the cancer; Alan never complained.

Alan continued, "It's just so encouraging each time he does it. There hasn't been one time I've seen him since I've been diagnosed that he hasn't taken the time to pray with me and for me." That was probably the most encouraging and profound gift that Chris ever could have given Alan.

One of the greatest joys in volunteering is that we are loving and serving other people. We get to learn their names and know their stories. Yes, at times we are serving them with food or help or teaching, but the most powerful thing we can do for them is to pray. James 5:13–15:

> Is any one of you in trouble? He should pray. Is anyone happy? Let him sing songs of praise. Is any one of you sick? He should call the elders of the church to pray over him and anoint him with oil in the name of the Lord. And the

prayer offered in faith will make the sick person well; the Lord will raise him up. If he has sinned, he will be forgiven.

Listen carefully to those you serve so you can figure out how to pray for them in the joyful times as well as in times of suffering. Be like Chris. Serve with the gift of prayer.

Questions for Reflection and Discussion

1. How have you seen God work through the power of prayer? What prayers have you seen God answer in your volunteer work, if you have already begun?

———————

2. How often do you pray about what you might do to use your gifts for God? How might you become more intentional about it? What are some habits or practices you can develop to make prayer a regular part of your volunteer service?

———————

3. Who are some of the people you are serving who might need prayer right now? Think about the past few weeks or months. What needs are you aware of? Write those down and commit to praying for them today.

CHAPTER 10

Ready, Get Set, Volunteer!

My two-year-old son, Greyson, is one of those children whom parents, teachers, and family members classify as "determined" or "spirited." All nice ways of saying he has a mind of his own. If he wants something, he'll figure out how to get it. If it takes a manipulative hug, he'll do it. If he needs to smile sweetly and say "please," he'll do that. Or if he thinks it might take a crabby face and swinging his arms to make his case, he'll occasionally do that as well. Parenting Greyson is like an amazing marathon; it doesn't ever seem to stop. There are the rewarding highs, and then there are moments when I think I might fall over in exhaustion.

What my husband and I love the most about Grey, though, is his excitement. When he finds a bug, you'd think he'd discovered gold. When he figures out he can spray someone with a hose, it's the best day he could ever imagine. Whenever he finds candles on the countertop for any reason, he bursts into, "Happy birfday, dear Geyson, happy birfday, dear Geyson, happy birfday to me." After all, shouldn't each day be a celebration for him? Excitement—he absolutely exudes it!

On a rather boring day, Greyson's daddy realized the boy needed something to do. In great dad fashion, he pulled off the couch cushions, turned up the music, set Greyson on the springs of the couch, and hollered, "Dance!" Daddy made sure to pad the floor with cushions to please Mom and save our son's good looks. Initially, Greyson was unsure about this new activity. He stood there for a while looking at Dad as the music blared. So Dad yelled again, "Dance, Greyson, dance," and slowly and skeptically he began moving his little feet. When Daddy shouted, "Good job," he started to shake his little behind. "Good job, Greyson, keep going!" And that was how our son turned into a dancing machine. Daily dance parties took place on our couch and usually concluded with "the worm," his best dance move to date.

Greyson's learning to dance reminds me of volunteering. Uncertain at the beginning, unsure of ourselves, we question whether we will really like it, whether we can really do it. Greyson took a risk and tried it. More important, he had a fan cheering him on, his daddy. We have a fan too. Our Daddy, the King of Kings and Lord of Lords, is cheering for us to jump in and be a part of this amazing, life-changing celebration called the church. We are the body of Christ, and we get to be a part of moving the mission of Jesus Christ forward.

God has wonderful and delightful things in store for you when you join his team and volunteer. He wants you to be a part. He is cheering, "Dance! Dance!" Will you do it? Will you join the best gathering ever, and will you risk learning the dance? You have a fan who will be cheering loudly to get you going, and if times of volunteering ever get long, hard, or even exhausting, listen for his voice: "Good job, keep going!"

Volunteering will change your life. But it won't be only your own life that is changed. Others will be transformed—some you won't even know about—because of what you do. If you want your life to have purpose, volunteer. If you want to make a difference, volunteer. If you want to change another person's life, volunteer. If you want to, yes, change the world, volunteer.

People need you. God wants you. Can you hear your biggest fan cheering?

Notes

1. Leslie B. Flynn, *19 Gifts of the Spirit* (Colorado Springs: David C. Cook, 1994).

2. United Health Group, "Volunteering Linked to Better Physical, Mental Health," news release, June 19, 2013, *http://www.unitedhealthgroup.com/newsroom/articles/feed/unitedhealth%20group/2013/0619healthvolunteering.aspx?*. The findings presented here are based on a national survey of 3,351 adults conducted by Harris Interactive, an international leader in population research and survey methodology. The survey was fielded between February 9 and March 18, 2013.

3. "The Health Benefits of Volunteering: A Review of Recent Research," issue brief, April 2007, *http://www.nationalservice.gov/sites/default/files/documents/07_0506_hbr_brief.pdf*.

4. Joanna Saisan, MSW, Melinda Smith, MA, and Gina Kemp, MA, "Volunteering and Its Surprising Benefits," Helpguide: A Trusted Non-Profit Resource, last updated December 2014, *http://www.helpguide.org/life/volunteer_opportunities_benefits_volunteering.htm*